FOREWORD BY: TRACEE GALES

BROKEN CRAYONS STILL COLOR

LEARN WHY LIFE IS A PAINTING, AND YOU ARE THE ARTIST

COMPILED BY: **DR. JESSICA BRAIDDEN**

Broken Crayons Still Color

By Dr. Jessica L. Braidden
©2024 Dr. Jessica L. Braidden

For information, contact:
MizCEO

Printed in the United States of America

CONTENTS

FOREWORD

by Tracee Gales

Useless, Worthless, Purposeless

These are just a few of the negative thoughts and emotions that oftentimes come as the result of those experiences that emotionally scar us, leaving us broken and in need of healing.

The powerfully transparent testimonies you are about to read are proof positive that no matter what life throws at you, you can be:

~ Broken and STILL useful

~ Broken and STILL powerful

~ Broken and STILL blessed

Broken Crayons Still Color will show you the value that comes when you stop looking at what and who is left and start looking for what's to come.

As you read these pages, let yourself believe that you will experience strength from your brokenness that will cause you to be strong enough to stand up to your future successes because YOUR story isn't over!

FROM BROKENNESS TO BREAKTHROUGH

by Monica Hunter

The term "broken" has an official definition but is subjective at the core of its essence. Why is that? The subjectivity is connected to how people respond to said brokenness. Some people allow their broken experiences to cripple them, while others utilize it to fuel their passions and ignite the fire that causes them to pursue greatness. This chapter will unpack how I used my brokenness to propel me into a space of self-reliance, resilience, perseverance, and self-love.

To understand the outcome, we must start from the beginning. Life's challenges caused me to believe that I was not and never would be enough. Growing up, I was constantly reminded that my cousins, friends, and foes were better than me. As a matter of fact, a patriarch in my family admonished me that there would always be someone better than our best. Now, I understand the impetus surrounding the impartation of collective humility. However, when I internalized those words, coupled with the fact that I was told I wasn't that great, my self-esteem began to suffer.

Case in point, I remember being in college and observing girlfriends discussing their beauty and "flyness" compared to other friend groups. I was appalled by their boastful sentiments, and when all eyes were on me to cast my stone of confidence, my learned humility caused me to soberly express, "I mean. I'm alright..." My friends were dumbfounded and didn't exactly understand how to respond. I also felt awkward because their melancholy reaction proved that I said something wrong. Instantly, each of them began to pour into me by exclaiming my beauty and that I should be comfortable boldly shouting it from the rooftop.

I, inorganically, agreed; we high-fived and moved on to preparing for a party. This experience taught me that I needed to balance humility and vanity. It was acceptable for me to exhibit self-confidence without walking in arrogance. However, I wasn't certain of how to consistently nurture that balance, so I slowly returned to being what I thought was humble but later realized it was a lack of self-worth.

Years later, I was married with children and worked as a teacher. I did well, but I knew I could always grow and develop. I chose to teach due to my encounter with a teacher in the third grade, Mrs. Calloway. She challenged me but loved and believed in me. Mrs. Calloway saw me in a space of chaos and trauma in which I was surrounded. By day, I was her model student. I cared for my siblings in the afternoon and evening and felt I didn't belong in my home. While in college, I decided that I must be the beacon of light for other children, as Mrs. Calloway was for me. I found my purpose in caring for and speaking life into my students, and that's precisely what I did.

After teaching for nearly four years, my principal empowered me to return to grad school to pursue an administrative certificate. Around the same time, a deacon at my church asked me if I'd ever considered attending school to become a principal. I immediately saw the correlation between the two conversations, which confirmed the next steps in my career, and I embraced it.

At the time, I was in a marriage that was less than healthy. I experienced physical, emotional, mental, and psychological abuse. I was a pastor's wife and had the weight of the ministry and my family on my shoulders. I knew that going back to school would allow me to leave a legacy of greatness for generations after me, but my mind wouldn't follow my heart. I felt inadequate and, again, not enough. I was an imposter. I was broken and didn't think I would or could get a job once I finished my program, so why even start? Then, I looked at my children, who became my "why."

They were and always will be my motivation. I became a mother at 16 and had two more by the time I was 22. Times were hard financially, and I did all I could to make ends meet. I watched neighborhood children for extra cash and even catered on weekends to supplement our income. I didn't know how much finishing the educational leadership program would impact my family, but I was willing to step out on faith.

I went back to school, and just like that, my husband had a stroke, and what was intended to be a semester break turned out to be a two-and-a-half-year break from classes. I eventually returned, finished the program, and was hired as an assistant principal two years later. In the meantime, I found myself divorced and a single mother with little support. I had a successful career, in my eyes, but I was still broken. Divorce stripped what little confidence I had, and I became comfortable in a space of grief. Then something happened. I heard motivational speaker Jim Rohn say, "We are the average of the five people we spend the most time with."

I reflected on my surroundings and realized I was enveloped by those who depended on me, but the support wasn't reciprocated. I performed a little experiment where I took a break from initiating communication with family and friends to determine the validity of my relationships. I quickly discovered that many of my friendships were one-sided. Then, I came across four women who were also broken, and we collectively decided to get back everything that life had stolen from us. A women's empowerment group called "The Get Back Girls" started just like that. We intentionally spoke into each others' lives and expanded that reach to women in the community.

Additionally, I led multiple initiatives within my school district and was promoted from assistant principal to principal, but I needed more. I pivoted from education and started a podcast called Silent No More, which brings insight into issues that plague the Black and Brown communities while providing resources for self-sufficiency, resilience, perseverance, and reliance. One of my main focuses was to bring awareness to the Black and Brown communities regarding mental health support while dismantling the shame therein.

I also shared my story by writing a book entitled, "Daughter in the Shadows," which is a memoir that shined a light on four prevalent themes that brought my life and community work together: childhood trauma, teenage pregnancy, living with domestic violence in silence, and life after divorce. This candid page-turner exposed my transparency to heal men, women, and children who have, are, or will experience varying facets of trauma in their lives.

I saw that there was still much to do for my family and the community, and I found my mission was to turn my pain into passion and my misery into ministry. Once I was healed enough to truly disaggregate my "why," I found my true purpose; I, as we all, can change the trajectory of our lives. We must see ourselves as God sees us and allow our experiences to fuel our destiny. Who has time to wallow in self-pity when there is a whole life of abundance and a colorful mark to make in our families, communities, and those whom God assigned us to impact? I understand that it all sounds easy, but one thing that is missed is the "how" after the "why."

First, reaching out for help in times of brokenness is vital. One reason I pride myself in educating the Black and Brown communities about mental health support is because it's necessary. There is nothing wrong with seeing a trusted licensed practitioner or life coach to see your situation differently. It's uncomfortable at first, but remember they've received training specific to support connected to every area of brokenness. Moreover, they will provide other resources such as self-help and care exercises, books to read, podcasts to listen to, etc. This work aids in changing your mindset, which brings me to my next point.

Your thought processes must shift from a space of lack to a place of abundance. I'm not talking about financial lack and abundance. I'm speaking of socio-emotional worth. You will not be whole if you can't see yourself in that manner. This is where affirmations come into play. A few years ago, my friend introduced me to quoting affirmations. I felt silly quoting them at first, but something clicked one day. I started to believe and see myself as the affirmations I spoke daily. My confidence miraculously shifted, and I started viewing every glass as half complete. At the same time, God began to show me the resources necessary to completely fill my cup, and the floodgates opened. Every goal I aspired to accomplish after it was written manifested in lightyear speed.

The third step is to "write the vision and make it plain ."Vision boards have become very popular in the past few years, and they work if faith matriculates the design. However, although vision boards have become popular and even fun, they are optional. You really need to write the goals you will pursue, develop a manageable action plan that is specific, measurable, attainable, reasonable, and time-specific, and walk out the plan. This part is easy and is not hocus pocus but biblical. Matthew 7:7 says ask and you will receive, seek and you will find, knock and the door will be open. You ask through spoken or written prayers. You seek by uncovering resources relative to your desires and using them to forge change. And, you knock by utilizing human capital and resources to bridge the gap to your success. This is why mentorship is so important.

Mentors provide knowledge and guidance that could prevent you from unnecessary pitfalls. Solid mentors share their successes and obstacles along with a blueprint of accomplishments. Selecting a mentor may seem intimidating to some, but remember, a good mentor will see your achievements as a figurative badge of honor. True leaders/mentors will see your potential and garner pride by participating in your process. It is imperative to engulf yourself with the success you want to acquire, and mentors are the key to unlocking your potential, power, and effective pursuit of greatness.

As a people, we are united and have everything we need to paint the picture of the divine sketched in His notepad of humanity. His desire for us is to prosper even as our soul prospers. He did not make mistakes and patterned our broken pieces to reveal beautifully designed mosaic artistry used to paint the picture of brokenness to wholeness. Tap into the supernatural power you now possess, change your mindset, get support, affirm yourself, write the vision, get a mentor, and be all you were destined to be. The choice is yours.

PERSEVERANCE THROUGH PAIN (MY JOURNEY WITH RHEUMATOID ARTHRITIS)

by Dr. Deidra Roussaw

Rheumatoid arthritis is a chronic autoimmune disease that affects the joints. In rheumatoid arthritis, the body's immune system attacks the joints, leading to inflammation and damage. This inflammation can cause pain, stiffness, and swelling in the joints, making it difficult to move and perform daily activities.

In the early stages of rheumatoid arthritis, the symptoms may be mild and may come and go. As the disease progresses, however, the symptoms can become more severe and can lead to joint deformities and disability. Rheumatoid arthritis can affect any joint in the body, but it most commonly affects the hands, wrists, and feet.

There is currently no cure for rheumatoid arthritis, but there are treatments that can help manage the symptoms and slow the progression of the disease. These treatments include medication, physical therapy, and lifestyle changes such as exercise and a healthy diet.

In 2004, I began experiencing symptoms associated with rheumatoid arthritis, but it wasn't until 2019 that I received an official diagnosis. This delay in diagnosis was due to my employment at a large hospital in Philadelphia. Had they correctly diagnosed me, I would have been forced to take medical leave.

For nearly fifteen years, I lived with the pain and discomfort of rheumatoid arthritis without knowing what was causing it. It affected my daily life, making simple tasks like opening jars or walking upstairs a struggle. I visited doctors and specialists, but no one could answer me.

In hindsight, the reason for this lack of diagnosis seems obvious. I worked for a hospital that was well aware of my symptoms, but they were hesitant to diagnose me with a chronic illness that would require time off work. The irony is not lost; I have worked in healthcare yet struggled to receive proper care.

It wasn't until 2019, after experiencing a particularly severe flare-up, that I was finally diagnosed with rheumatoid arthritis. While the news was not what I wanted to hear, it was a relief to finally have a clear understanding of what was causing my pain. I was able to begin treatment and make lifestyle changes that helped manage my symptoms.

Looking back, I can't help but feel frustrated by the years of uncertainty and pain that could have been avoided with an earlier diagnosis.

Despite the pain I experienced, I persevered for the sake of my family, job, business, education, and ministry. Many people envied me for the success they saw, but few knew the challenges I had to overcome to achieve it all. I worked full-time at a hospital five days a week, managed our family business, and led a ministry for wives.

The days were long, and the work was demanding. But I refused to let my physical pain hold me back. I had a family to help support, a business to maintain, a ministry to lead, and I was a leader at my church. It was not always easy, but I was determined to succeed.

People looked at me and saw the success that I had achieved. They envied me for it, thinking that my life was easy. But they didn't know my struggles to get to where I was. They didn't see the long hours, the physical pain, and the sacrifices I had made along the way.

I had learned to persevere through it all, even when things seemed impossible. I had developed a strength and resilience that I never knew I had. And while it was not easy, I knew it was all worth it. Through it all, I learned that anything was possible with hard work, dedication, and a lot of faith.

.In 2017, I underwent bilateral knee replacements. Leading up to my surgery, I was unable to walk for four months. Fortunately, my husband and daughter were there for me every step of the way. My husband prepared most of our meals, did the house cleaning, paid bills, and took care of other household chores. My daughter was also my primary support system, taking me to all my appointments, running errands, completing paperwork, and providing me with entertainment when needed. My grandchildren were my runners, always eager to help in

At the hospital, I worked tirelessly to provide the best care possible for the patients. I was dedicated to my job and did everything in my power to make a difference in the lives of those I served. But my work did not end when I left the hospital. In fact, it was just beginning.

As soon as I finished my shift, I would rush to our family business to help oversee its operations. We had worked hard to build our business, and I was committed to ensuring its success. I worked long hours, ensuring every detail was handled, from managing our finances to supervising our employees.

Despite the demands of my job and our family business, I was also passionate about serving others through our ministry for wives. I dedicated my time and energy to helping wives in our community grow in their faith and relationships. It was important work, and I felt honored to be a part of it.

Through it all, I had to push through the pain. It was difficult, but I knew giving up was not an option. My family, job, business, and ministry depended on me. And so, I persisted with the help of the Lord.

any way they could. Together, this team provided the support and care I needed to get through this difficult time.

Looking back, I remember a warning my mother gave me when I was younger. She found my coat hidden near the dryer vent after a night out at the club because I didn't want the coat to get in the way of me dancing on the dance floor with my girls. She stated, "If I didn't take care of myself, arthritis would catch up with me!" I didn't pay much attention to her warning at the time because I was young and thriving, but now I realize how right she was. My arthritis has had a profound impact on my life. Every morning, I wake up not knowing whether I'll be able to walk or need to spend the day in bed. The process is painful, but I keep the purpose hidden in my heart and push through the pain.

In 2019, I was finally diagnosed with rheumatoid arthritis after moving to a new city. I immediately began practicing meditating on the Lord, which has helped me immensely. I often speak about my experience with rheumatoid arthritis to others to show that despite having the disease, it does not have to control my life. On days when the pain is too much to bear, I turn to prayer, pain medication, and rest. I choose not to rely solely on pain medication, as I am aware of the dangers of addiction. Instead, I opt for injections, which seem to help.

My ankles and wrists are the joints most affected by arthritis, which forced me to take a step back and reevaluate my priorities. I realized that I needed to lighten my workload to avoid exacerbating my symptoms. This led me to create a team of ambassadors in 2020. With many of the wives taking over specific tasks, it gives me the freedom I desire to take care of myself. Now, I can coach and mentor them while focusing on researching, resetting, and relaxing.

The outcome of my painful purpose has been transformational. My struggles taught me to prioritize my health and focus on what truly matters. I have developed a stronger connection with my family and have discovered the importance of building a support network. By sharing my experiences with others, I aim to inspire and educate them on overcoming their own challenges.

Ultimately, my painful purpose has taught me that life is entirely of obstacles, but how we face them defines who we are. Instead of letting my illness control my life, I have decided to take control and use it as an opportunity to grow and help others. I am joyful about how far I've come and what I've been able to achieve despite the challenges I face.

Through my journey with rheumatoid arthritis, I have learned the importance of self-care and taking care of my body. I've also learned the value of having a supportive team and community around me. My husband, daughter, and grandchildren have been my rocks, and I am grateful for their love and support.

I have discovered a newfound purpose in mentoring and coaching others as I continue this path. By sharing my story and experiences, I aim to inspire others struggling with chronic illnesses or any other challenges they face. I encourage them to keep pushing forward, even when it feels impossible.

Despite the pain and struggles that come with my illness, my body may feel broken or broken down at times, but the Lord still allows me to operate with my gifts and talents. I am determined to live a fulfilling and meaningful life as a believer. I may not be able to do everything I used to, but I have found new ways to contribute and make a difference in the lives of others.

ABOUT DR. DEIDRA ROUSSAW

Dr. Deidra Roussaw is a licensed and ordained minister, certified relationship coach, leadership expert, certified mentor, best-selling author, TEDx & international speaker, honored by President Obama with the prestigious Presidential Lifetime Achievement Award,visionary, blogger, and the founder of TrulyWed Wives®, a wives leadership ministry offering wives retreats, seminars & workshops. She has a degree in business from South New Hampshire University. Dr. Deidra is a Certified Sandals & Beaches WeddingMoons Specialist and a Cruise Specialist offering pleasurable resources and romantic exposure for couples to strengthen and enhance their marriages.

Dr. Deidra is the brand specialist for the Wives on Fire Escapements, Wives Night Out ~ Slumber Parties by the Signature Wife Coach and TrulyWed Wives Society of Ambassadors.

She is committed to providing exuberant experiences that will invoke passion and devotion to the sanctity of marriage.

She is the author of "No Wife Left Behind" and a book she compiled with over 50 other wives, "Wives on Fire!" She hosts a monthly Wives on Fire Mastermind and a weekly Wives on Fire Bible Study. She is honored to be one of hundreds of women contributing authors to Black CEO.

She teaches wives on how to create a luxurious WifeStyle, how to be their husbands GOOD THING & mentor WifeCEO's on how to balance business and marriage as a WifePrenuers.

She is the co-founder of TWOgether Marriages, hosts an annual Marriage on Fire Retreat ~ Marriage Sailabration, a monthly "Date Night Tour & Experience" Editor-in-

Chief for the *Marriage on Fire Magazine*, magazine publisher and the host of the Marriage on Fire Radio Show & Podcast alongside her husband, Dr. Dwight Roussaw.

Dr. Deidra is a graduate and alumni of Success Mastery Coaching under the leadership of Dr. Stacia and Arianna Pierce and David Tutera Mentorship Program.

Her Wife Verse~ "A wife of noble character is her husband's crown" ~Proverbs 12:4

BROKEN CRAYONS STILL COLOR

by Tiara M. Tucker, M.S.

One of the most popular passages in the Bible is Psalm 23, a psalm of David. In the New International Version (NIV), verses 1-6 read as follows:

The Lord is my shepherd; I lack nothing. He makes me lie down in green pastures. He leads me beside quiet waters. He refreshes my soul. He guides me along the right paths for his name's sake. Even though I walk through the darkest valley, I will fear no evil, for you are with me; your rod and your staff, they comfort me. You prepare a table before me in the presence of my enemies. You anoint me head with oil; my cup overflows. Surely, your goodness and love will follow me all the days of my life, and I will dwell in the house of the Lord forever.

This passage took on a different meaning when I had the supernatural opportunity to experience it for myself in 2019.

In 2019, I felt like I was secretly living someone else's foreign life. Although I was doing my best to smile, show up, and pour into others, I somehow became empty. I knew I wasn't the same smiling, loud-talking, energetic Tiara that people associated with. After hiding it for as long as I could, others started to notice.

During this part of my journey in life, I felt like I was living on two sides of the spectrum at the same time. I was miserable, but I was living my best life while some of my personal and professional dreams were coming true. I was confused, but I also thought what I wanted in life was clear. I was mentally and emotionally exhausted, but I was physically rested because all I wanted to do was lay in my bed and sleep. I was hopeless, but I was optimistic. I was depressed, but I was still using my voice and platforms to empower and inspire others.

Deep down in my core, I knew my dreams, the plans for my life, and the impact I could make in the lives of others were still there and were screaming for me to snap back. I just didn't know how. I was numb and just going through the motions until I couldn't even move to get out of my bed some days. When I forced myself to crawl out of bed and cry to work, I felt invisible, and I don't even think people noticed when I didn't come in. I had sunken so low to this foreign place that I didn't know how to show up. I was broken, and I knew I needed to get back for myself and those around me. I was lost and yearning to be found.

So, I decided to take a break from my corporate career, my Tiara PR Network business, my Speak That! Movement organization and my personal life, and I do the only thing I feel led to do: take a break to escape. I wasn't sure what I needed to do or where to go, but I knew I needed to leave and be all alone to get closer to God and get Tiara back.

One late night, I woke up out of my sleep, and an image of Colorado was vividly clear to me. I had never been there before, but I always wanted to go. I immediately pulled out my phone and looked up a flight from Dallas to Denver. To my surprise, my favorite airline had a flight for less than $50 one-way departing on Saturday, June 1, 2019, so I decided that would be my escape destination and departure date.

I wasn't concerned about my return flight because I had no clue how long I needed to be away, so I only focused on getting there and taking it day by day. I looked up lodging options and found what appeared to be—and what ended up being—a perfect room in a cozy, highly-rated Airbnb. I secured the room for the maximum number of days allowed, booked a rental car, and started looking into things to do while there.

I told my manager I needed to take some time off of work – the entire month of June, to be exact – without letting him know why to protect my privacy. Surprisingly, he approved my month-long request without questions because I had plenty of paid time off. I let my family know I was escaping but never told anyone where I was going until I was on the plane ready to depart. I asked that they not reach out to me while away because I needed this time to get me back. They all respected and appreciated it.

A TURN OF EVENTS

To my surprise, a turn of unexpected events happened just days before my escape. I was feeling defeated, down, and depressed, yet extremely excited about my upcoming soul-searching trip. I decided to take a walk in my neighborhood, which has one of the most gorgeous hidden jewel lakes, bridges, trees, and a golf course I had ever seen in a neighborhood.

As I was walking and listening to an inspirational speaker on my phone, I decided to just sit down in the green pastures beside the quiet waters. The next thing I knew, the wind was lightly blowing the tall trees around me, and an indescribable peace came over me that made me lie down. I have no clue how long I was lying down because I felt like I drifted away physically, mentally, spiritually, and emotionally. I was awakened by my neighborhood's groundskeeper, who saw me lying down and came to check on me.

When he woke me up and learned I was ok, I knew God was using him to speak to me, as he had done multiple times before (that's for another book). He started sharing

Scripture with me. When he left, I got up and knew God
had worked a miracle on me, and my soul was refreshed!
I didn't feel like the same person anymore. I felt like God
healed me and did something new in me even before
I left town to get closer to Him. He showed me that I
didn't need to seek Him because He is omnipresent.

The next few days leading up to my trip felt drastically
better; however, I knew I wasn't supposed to cancel my
plans. From the moment I got to the airport on that
first Saturday of June to when I returned to Dallas, I
felt God's presence like never before. I knew without a
shadow of a doubt that His presence was with me the
entire time.

While away on what turned out to be one of the most
serene trips of my life, I removed myself from social
media and turned my ringer off. I created a prayer closet
on my Airbnb and spent my mornings and nights there
with God. I went to church on Sunday morning and
felt like angels surrounded me. Before I walked into the
church, I was greeted as if a halo was over my head. An
"angel" greeter prayed for me before I walked into the

sanctuary, and she stayed in touch after I left town. At church, the pastor was preaching about mindfulness, a concept I never heard of, but it felt like the sermon was created for me.

Throughout my trip, mindfulness kept popping up. I practiced mindfulness yoga with an instructor at the gorgeous Garden of the Gods, where I saw God's creations in another way. I participated in a mindfulness meditation where I learned to find peace within no matter what is going on around me. I participated in a mindfulness hike, in which I courageously hiked to the top of a mountain only to forget how, just days before, I was at my lowest valley. That hike taught me that no matter how challenging an obstacle, God is there to help.

THE TRANSFORMATIONAL RETURN

Escaping from everything to get closer to God was the best thing that could have ever happened to me. When I came back to Dallas, I was a renewed person. My mind was clear, my energy increased, and my desire to go all in on my dreams and goals was at an all-time high. I used the rest of June to stay focused. I immediately created a prayer closet in one of my bedrooms that I still go into to spend quiet time with God. I also was so intrigued by the concept of mindfulness that I earned a Certificate in Mindfulness, which has helped me to get through many more situations in life and help others.

During my break, I committed to my career, organization, dreams, goals, and mental health. From June 2019 to March of 2023, I can proudly proclaim I've had some of the most significant accomplishments in my life, including Growing my personal Tiara PR Network and Speak That! Movement brands; landing a dream role with my Fortune 50 employer (that I have since resigned from after 18 years to do my own thing); reaching 6-figures; receiving multiple prestigious awards and honors; landing numerous speaking engagements; launching new endeavors; and building new relationships with supportive people. My efforts have touched more lives than I could have ever imagined.

KEEP ON COLORING

My ever-growing relationship with God and myself has grown tremendously since my break to escape. I now know what it feels like to be broken and that only God can make you whole again. Even today, I still have moments when I feel like I am losing my mind during recurring battles of anxiety, doubt, fear, self-diagnosed ADHD paralysis, or when resources appear to be limited. During these trying times, I pause and reflect on my real-life psalm of David's experience.

I am reminded that the Lord is my shepherd; I lack nothing. I can keep on coloring. I lean in on the thought that He makes me lie down, leads me, and refreshes my soul in only a way He can. I can keep on coloring. He guides me along the right paths when I feel lost or want to give up. I can keep on coloring. When I am faced with walking through the darkest valley, I will fear no evil because I have already climbed the highest mountain with Him by my side. I feel a supernatural comfort reminding me that I can continue coloring.

No matter what you are going through or how broken you may feel along your journey, I encourage you to fail to escape if you must, but just keep on coloring. Even if it is hard to believe there is hope at times, always remember that your cup will overflow, and goodness and love will follow you all the days of your life, so you just keep on coloring...

FORGIVENESS

by Shamala Stidham

Growing up, I was always the one with the bad attitude, quick to fight, beyond angry all the, etc. As I got older, it also continued through my adult years. Although I put on a confident face, I was insecure and damaged. I married at 25, and I started out being the abuser mentally,physically, and verbally. It was soon flipped, and he became the abuser. I was beaten, shot at, dragged across the floor by my hair, ran off the road, I mean, you name it.

Growing up, I watched my mother get beat by her boyfriend for almost six years. I vowed to never allow a man to hit me, and I did just that for about 13 years. I've been on this healing journey for about 4 to 5 years, but in the last year or so, I've been on a spiritual journey. I no longer wanted to be the angry, attitude-having chick.

I battled with depression for years, and I was exhausted from the constant battle. I've never known what being truly happy felt like, and I was ready to find out. I was ready for peace in my life, heart, and in my mind. In 2017, right around the time I started my healing journey and wrote my first book. I had to open up wounds that I suppressed all my life. I had to get to the root of all my anger and reckless choices.

First, let me state that I was born to a 13-year-old girl and given to my grandparents to raise as their child. When they both passed away, my mother had to become a mother to me and the baby boy she was pregnant with. Barely 20 years old at this time, this young girl had to become a mother to a sassy five 1/2-year-old little girl who thinks they're sisters.

She and the father of the child she was pregnant with split early in the pregnancy. About a month before she gave birth to her baby boy, she met a man, and things between them moved quickly. By the time the baby boy was four months old, they moved in together.

This is where the root of my anger and poor choices started. The guy started molesting me while my mother worked nights. It went from rubbing his hand against my private area to laying on top of me and rubbing his private against mine, and from him inserting his penis into my mouth and saying that he was teaching me early.

I was about eight years old when I decided to tell my mother what he was doing to me, and I had the courage to do this right in front of him. He told her I was lying, and I was told to go sit my lying ass down. That night, I was brutally raped by him as punishment for opening up my mouth. This happened for years. She eventually left him, but it wasn't because of what was happening to me.

For years, I held this hatred for my mother. Our relationship was a rollercoaster. On April 10, 2010, my mother had a stroke while she was at church. She was rushed to the hospital, where I was told to make funeral arrangements. Almost losing her so suddenly softened my heart towards my mother. I always loved my mother and would do anything in the world for her despite the hatred I held for her.

I started letting go of that aggression I had towards her and provided her with the best life I possibly could. Where I am today, I am in the forgiveness phase. I study with a spiritual advisor, and I'm learning about energy, chakras, and reprogramming my mind. I'm also fasting, praying, and meditating. Which is how I genuinely forgive my mother. I love her more, and although I don't understand why I wasn't protected, I understand she was lost in a world with no mother nor father and survived and raised now three children.

On this journey, I've seen some of my mistakes due to having hatred in my heart. I tried so hard not to be my mother that I made similar choices. She had a child by a man that raped me, and I married and had two children by a man that molested my oldest daughter. I wish I had gotten help when I was younger, but that hurt is growing into the woman God intended me to become.

I now genuinely love myself and wholeheartedly forgive my mother. My mother is dying; she is now doing hospice from home. She will leave this earth in peace, knowing that she was beyond love. I was fed up with the hurt little girl looking to be saved. I was ready for this beautiful butterfly to emerge, and she's blossoming. " I think the first step is to understand that forgiveness does not exonerate the perpetrator. Forgiveness liberates the victim.

It's a gift you give yourself," Bishop T. D. Jakes.

LIFE AS A BUSINESS WOMAN OF COLOR

by Monique Johnson

Feeling accomplished makes me feel purposeful. As far back as I can remember, I was always goal-oriented, whether that came from completing all the brain teasers in the puzzle books,putting together a jigsaw puzzle, or just wanting to have excellent grades so my parents didn't question my extracurricular behaviors.

Whether something came easy or was a challenge, I put my all into accomplishing it to make sure that the end result was as close to perfect as it could be. It had gotten to the point where I started to recognize that I don't take time to celebrate the wins that I accomplish. I only focus on checking off a box and moving to the next goal to accomplish.

Why do I associate completing tasks and recognition with being successful? When your education and career life have always been on an upward trajectory, it was a mental and emotional struggle when I had to maneuver and figure out what I wanted to do next after my favorite job closed. Starting your own business is great when you have a vision of how to give to society what may be lacking. It is difficult when you don't know how to maneuver through society.

I, personally, struggle with the art of networking in order to advance my motive. I am the type where my work ethic and building relationships have always allowed me to advance, even when I wasn't looking to. Opportunities came up that I was able to take advantage of. When you own your own business, networking, and marketing are part of your business advancement and survival. This is one of my biggest struggles.

Even though I have been goal-oriented, it has always come from a genuine place, and I believe in being humble. "Bragging" on a service that I can provide just doesn't seem humble. So, the question bids itself to ask: Is networking and marketing a struggle because of my belief or is it a struggle because it is something that I was not taught how to do, so it is a skill that I don't have?" This is an area where I always feel defeated.

I also struggle with how to show up to others. From everyone telling me, even down to personality tests, I show up as a task-driven person, which is not what I want to give off to others. I want the passion of why I give my all to be the first thing people see, but this never is the case. I don't know how to make it the focal point, which is probably why I thrive off of building relationships with people, so they know how genuine my heart is. I don't want to be this bossy Black woman, and I try very hard to scale her back.

When I scale her back, I end up being quiet and not wanting my personality to shine through until I feel "likable," and then I feel like I can pull out the task-driven part of myself. I truly care for people and am involved in so much professionally, spiritually, and personally, because I always say it is not just about me. But what do I do with this part of myself that I deny all the time because I don't want to come off "too strong" to others, which then turns them away from building a relationship with me, which then hurts any future opportunities that can arise? If only I knew how to make my second trait my first trait and vice versa. Maybe this is my challenge to continually work on. Not only is not being this bossy Black woman a struggle with how I show up to others, but I also struggle with the professional look, especially being a woman of color. I don't wear makeup, I was never taught how to wear makeup, and I am not interested in learning how to wear makeup.

I can count on one hand the number of times I wore makeup between my teen years and adulthood. I also struggle with very bad acne, and I have little interest in learning what I feel are complicated facial regiments to correct the acne. I am also not the most fashionable person. I do not know how to walk in heels for a long period of time, meaning more than an hour. I dress for comfort rather than presentation.

I have natural hair, which doesn't always hold in style, especially when exercising is a part of my lifestyle. In a society where there are professional physical standards, this is an extreme challenge for me. I recognize this and feel self-conscious about it. In further reflection on this, I realize it is because I do not want to give time and mental energy to these processes when I have so many other things that demand my time and energy.

I am also not genuinely interested in makeup and heels, so I question myself if I focus on it. Is it because I am only satisfying society's view of what I should look like? Would I then be denying another part of myself to fit in? I focus on showing up to spaces with a presentable natural look, especially with my hair, but it can only go so far if I am exercising. I don't feel desirable, even professionally, in showing up to spaces.

I have been a provider since I was 14 years old. I was homeless in high school and still provided for my brother and my mother. Now, I am providing for my mother and my toddler son. Being a mom of a toddler is one of my biggest challenges as a businesswoman because I still need to show up for him. I thought that there would be two of us showing up for him, but since it did not happen that way, I know that it is my ultimate responsibility to put him first, after God, in his growing and learning years. Because I have this provider role in my family and with my ex-husband, it drains me.

In order to set boundaries, I have to continually say to myself: People will suck you dry, whether they recognize it or not. This helps me a lot. I even have to set boundaries with my son because I recognize that even though he is a high priority, he is also not allowed to drain me. I set boundaries with church activities because sometimes the action ends up being, if you want something done, give it to a busy person. I used to feel guilty if I did not fulfill what was asked of me, but now I know my capacity and where I can apply more intentional growth without overwhelming myself. These are teachable moments that I am constantly communicating.

I also find it hard sometimes to maneuver between the people who held you down when you didn't have anything but are currently not in the same growth process as you. I feel like I don't fit in with this "sophisticated" business crowd, but I also don't fit in with my old life because I am not the same person from last year. I am still trying to reconcile this because I love building relationships, but I also want to feel comfortable.

I named all these struggles, but what are the glamorous parts of being a successful business woman, and why do I continue to pursue it? It fulfills me and makes me feel purposeful. I was once told that a priority doesn't necessarily make something your purpose, and with deep reflection, I truly buy into this ideology. I know I have more to give, regardless of what is going on in my life. Sometimes, I need to slow down or take a break, but that doesn't take the end goal away.

There are still small steps that can be done in the midst of other priorities and/or distractions. I need to SHOW UP, even when I don't know how. I believe that if you put yourself in a position to reach a goal, opportunities will come, even if they have nothing to do with the goal you had in mind.

I have been choosing myself for the past two years, and I will continue to use this year to choose me. I have other personal goals in life that have nothing to do with business where I had to choose myself, like taking up dance classes, investing in my house to fellowship with others, and intentional spiritual growth.

I still color because you have to put yourself in a position to receive blessings. I still color because that is the difference between successful versus significant. I still color because regardless of all these "broken" parts of me, I want to add to the beautiful picture of the world.

BUILDING A BUSINESS, WHILE STILL BEING AN EMPLOYEE

by Kendra Johnson

Most people dream of what they want to be in childhood. I am no different. I knew I wanted to help people. As a teenager, I thought I would be a doctor. As I got older, I realized I wanted to support those dealing with trauma.

The thought of owning a business wasn't even a thought until I was twenty years old. No one I knew personally owned a business as a child except maybe the candy ladies who sold items out or their homes. Therefore, having a business was not something I thought was attainable. As children, my siblings and I were told the traditional "Go to college and make enough money to take care of yourself." The principles of business and what it takes to own one were like a foreign language to me.

A supervisor, who was like a big sister, introduced me to the book "Who Moved My Cheese" by Spencer Johnson while I was working at a childcare facility. That book was the first of many that would spark my curiosity about owning something for myself. Later on, much later, it would come to fruition as a family business.

Before that happened, I went on the traditional path and went to college. College was the only way I knew to succeed and escape my reality of being in poverty, living on the south side of Chicago, and providing as a single parent close to minimum wage. Undergraduate turned to Graduate school and a master's degree turned into eight years of working in the social work world before the opportunity to start a business in 2020. That would be twelve years after the original idea was planted. God created the opportunity and put the right people in place to start a business.

I did not go to school for business. I wasn't taught business principles in childhood. My business partner was not taught these things either. We did not have investors or startup money. We did not even know how to create a business plan, let alone apply for an LLP (Limited Liability Partnership).

Naturally, we still worked full-time jobs and worked our business a quarter of the time starting out. How does one work as an employee and run a business full-time? How do you split your time? How do you work on your own purpose and dream as much as working on someone else's? How do you make the decision to work your business full-time and not worry about living the life you are accustomed to? I could not answer those questions in 2020 when we started and found myself exhausted. When you are on the outside looking in, people look like they are thriving in their business and have everything in order. No one told me about all the challenges of having a business.

The first thing I had to learn was to change my mindset from employee to business owner when working my business. I had to realize every hour toward my business was for myself and my growth. Changing your mindset when you have been on the employee side of the business world for over 15 years is a challenge. I had to understand my why, purpose, motivation, and desire to start my own business. Creating and doing an inventory of how you are managing your business is key. I was honest with myself when I was not doing a great job at my business. It was and still is hard to admit sometimes. As an employee, I made sure my clients were supported, and progress notes were done on time. I had to learn to give that same energy and dedication to my business. I acknowledged my struggle with my business and created a plan to do better the next week.

The second thing you learn is that you need key people around you to support you in areas where you're not as knowledgeable. Jesus had 12 disciples who helped spread his message around the world. He didn't do it alone. If you need a mentor, a business partner, an accountant, or a business consultant, take the time to find trustworthy people who can join you on this journey.

As an accountant or a business consultant, you should take time to locate trustworthy people to take the journey with you. This can take some time. Remember, it took 12 years for the right people to be aligned with the purpose and vision of MK-TI Social Work Consulting and 14 years to create the Resources and Opportunities Women Need.

Not everyone you start with will continue the journey, and that is okay. Holding people accountable and trusting they will do what they say can be very stressful. Make sure you set boundaries, have someone trustworthy (another business owner would be ideal) to bounce ideas off, and know how to have difficult, courageous conversations. Difficult, courageous conversations will happen often.

The third thing you learn is to set realistic expectations and measurable goals. It's easy to see full -time business owners and get discouraged by your own productivity. It took three years to be in the space we are in today. In the beginning, I had six to twelve-month goals that probably were more like two-to-three-year goals. I overwhelmed myself and had to go slower. I still needed to be healthy, take care of a teenager, and work to keep a certain level of income.

Everything that has been built was built while still being an employee, and I had to start celebrating the little successes to really appreciate the big ones. It is possible to build a business while being an employee. Understand that it won't be easy, but it is worth your time. It does not look like the glitz and glamor of what you see on social media, and it is not always the same productivity level as a full-time business owner.

Changing your mindset, finding your key people, and setting reasonable goals for your business will keep you going when you are ready to quit.

SILENCE SPEAKS VOLUMES

by Dr. Jessica Reese

If I am honest with myself, I spent my childhood and most of my young adult years doing what others told me to do and what they wanted me to do. From the clothes I wore, the foods I ate, to the music playing through my earphones, very seldom were my opinions solicited before decisions were made that affected me.

I have the distinction of growing up in the South. Yes, I've been a Georgia peach before, and it was the popular, trendy thing to be or hold on the television screen. Before there was the Real Housewives of Atlanta, there was the Real Southern Belles of Georgia...well, at least in my mind. One thing about women from the South is that we are often labeled as meek, mild, and soft-spoken. We are to keep the house and family operating smoothly as the man of the house goes out to bring home the bacon. We are believed to know how and want to cook, take care of the kids, take care of our man, keep a clean house, and always be prepared to provide that good ol' southern hospitality at any given moment.

While all that may be true, desired, preferred, and expected, this Georgia peach had a few more ingredients to add to the recipe of being a woman from the South.

I already told you that decisions were made for me. No, they were not always voiced or directly communicated, but they were what I would like to call implied decisions. You know, those implied decisions, the ones that said everything without one word ever being spoken or written. I believe the new generation would say I was influenced. Wait, so does that mean my family and friends were influencers before being an "influencer" became a thing? Were they the "Original Influencers"? Although it is a rhetorical question, the answer is yes.

Let's be honest: from pre-K to grade 12, one thing should be the focus of every child's life - education. Everything else, from friends, jobs, sports, extracurricular activities, and the list goes on, should be a second or a minor focus. Education is the key, the master key that unlocks opportunities, and I had that lesson instilled in me from a very young age. So, when it was time to graduate high school and apply to college, the idea of doing anything other than that had to be silenced. Who did I think I was to entertain any other option than college? Now the question was, which one? Would I follow in the footsteps of family members older than me, or would I mute the voice of fear and apply to Spelman College? Decisions...decisions...and one had to be made.

My campus visit to Spelman College sealed the deal for me. I knew I needed to be there. It was the culture for me. It was the sisterhood for me. It was the unapologetic illumination of excellence for me. It was the audacity to believe that I embodied what it meant to be a Spelman Woman.

Not long after becoming a Spelmanite, I became the girl in the dorms doing everybody's hair. I know, I know, yes, I was studying to earn my degree, but I was also washing, drying, wrapping, slicking down, finger-waving, and curling some hair. I had a (self-imposed) responsibility to make sure my fellow Spelmanites looked good...and they did, as I have always loved affecting how a woman sees herself when she looks in the mirror.

After graduation, I did what I was "supposed to do." I went to work to work for someone else. I took a highly compensated position with a Fortune 5 company, where I quickly climbed the corporate ladder. I was a beast, not to toot my own horn, but I took advantage of the opportunities to learn, grow, teach, and excel. I didn't know what the future held, but wherever I ended up, I knew I would have had great, top-notch training that armed me with transferable skills to any industry.

A few years later my husband and I were blessed to become pregnant. After being placed on bed rest for the majority of my pregnancy, for the first time in my life I was able to unmute my dreams, ideas and sit with my thoughts. I was finally able to ask myself the hard questions and get this, I was also finally able to answer them.

There I was on the cusp of starting a new chapter of my life - motherhood. I had never been a mother before. I had never had the responsibility of caring for someone 24 hours, 7 days a week. Everything I was, they would see. Everything I was not, they would feel. Everything I regretted, they would sense.

In reality, I was not really starting a new chapter; unbeknownst to me, I was starting a new book. I was evolving into the woman who was done playing the stage help when I was the main character. I took my power and activated what would become a beauty brand empire; I enrolled in cosmetology school. Yes, this Spelman graduate, a highly compensated executive, left corporate America and took my career ladder off their building and placed it on her own building...by 2022, it has been on seven buildings, to be exact. Yes, tooting my horn again.

Silence speaks volumes. I did not have to wonder if family and friends understood my decision to leave corporate America to enroll in cosmetology school. No, no one ever said anything mean or bad; they just did not say anything. It was the silence that was unsettling. It was the silence that planted seeds of doubt, confusion, isolation, and defeat. The silence was deafening. I was tossed and turned into this sea of emotions, but I stayed in my boat. I kept praying. I kept rowing. I kept remembering my why. Did I want to give up? Yes. Did I want to throw in the towel? Yes. Did I want to hear congratulations? Yes. Did I want to see my posts shared by them across social media platforms? Yes. But I could not let any of those things stop me. I learned that the reason I noticed the silence was because it was from the people in the front rows of my life. I had to learn to listen for the faint cheers and hoorays because those were from the people furthest away...strangers and people who arrived in the midst of my success, seated in the last rows and balconies of my life. They do not care what they missed; they are just glad they made it to see you win.

If you live for the applause of others, you will die from their silence. Take your power and turn up your volume.

GRACE THROUGH THE STORM: LESSONS IN FAITH AND RESILIENCE

by Dr. Lakisha Irby

There comes a time when you have to stop and thank God for every experience in your life. Romans 8:28 says, "And we know that all things work together for good to them that love God, to them who are the called according to his purpose." This means all things, whether good or bad, work together for your Divine purpose. One thing we have to know is that God knows the beginning all the way to the end. All of it is going to work in your favor.

I personally have been mistreated by those who were supposed to walk with me on this journey, but because of God's grace and mercy, every betrayal, lie, and weapon formed did not prosper but worked in my favor. God knows the heart of every matter. He knows how to get to the root of a thing. Even though it may be hard at times to keep your heart in check, don't do them like they did you.

One of my biggest mistakes as a business owner was to become friends with my staff. Even though I helped pay bills, sowed into their lives, allowed them to fellowship in my home, and blessed them and their children, I know that I did all of it with a pure heart. When you do things with a pure heart, at the end of the day, you can sleep peacefully at night. There have been a series of incidents that transpired due to a bitter and dangerous ex who harassed several members of my staff and clients out of jealousy. Because of the harassment from this ex and one of his many girlfriends, which was totally out of my control, the staff turned on me when I started to get the law involved. In the end, the people who I thought were employees, as well as supportive friends, actually turned out to be my enemies with wicked agendas.

They were people who were harboring ill will and intent based on untruths and false rumors. These women came to my place of employment with erratic behavior that shocked me because I thought we were, first and foremost, friends. I learned a powerful lesson through that entire ordeal, and that was to keep business and personal separate. In that, I found out these girls were jealous but also thought they were coming back to my place of employment by going through a family member. I'm thankful I serve a God that doesn't leave His children in the dark and ignorant. I served them with a no-trespassing judgment due to the disrespect and dishonor of myself on my property. All of this craziness from these girls occurred in front of another staff member and business associates. I sent the no-trespassing notice, and it hurt to have to do so. In all of my doing, I've had to learn that when God shows you a person's character along with their intent, you can take it to the bank! There was no question in what God continuously showed me about these girls and their intent to destroy my business. When people don't have anything to lose, they don't care about tearing up your stuff. When there is no stock in the assignment, and the person has gone rogue, you can forget about them caring about the state of your success.

I always attribute a part of my success to the fact

I sowed into another man's business before God began to bless me on my own. I worked for an event planning company while pregnant. At the time, I had moved from Georgia back to South Carolina and was then separated from my husband. I treated that business as if it were my own. I took my job seriously as a Day of Coordinator. In that position, I was partly responsible for the day prior to an event and the day of coordination. I devoted several years to that position during the remainder of my pregnancy and for several years until my assignment was done. After I served in that company, the owner started to slander my name. This wasn't an uncommon act by this woman; it was something she frequently did to people who left the company, even if it was on good terms. I always treated her with love and treated the company as my own, but when it was time to depart to focus on my own growing companies, the love wasn't reciprocated. I felt slighted in many ways because I knew I gave that position my all to be lied to in the end. I went to work with swollen feet, had to have a babysitter for my young child, and also sacrificed time with my own family to commit to events out of my loyalty to her company.

A few short years later, the owner was accused of embezzling money from several clients by not paying vendors for upcoming events. Needless to say, I was there at the beginning of her business, from me hiring her as the day coordinator for my own wedding to the downfall, and today, a nonexistent business. Her downfall literally only took a few short years to occur, but it taught me to give honor where honor is due. If you choose to dishonor where honor is due, or in her case, choose to lie to those who helped to build a business by reaching the level of success it did, God has a way of humbling you rather quickly. She had an unchecked heart issue that God warned her about before I came along. Not dealing with those issues within her heart caused her to lose the thing God wanted to bless her with. One thing people have to understand is that the price of greatness is not about being friends; it's about handling business God's way. It's about completing God's assignment first. His Word says, "If any man comes to me and hates not his father, mother, and wife, and children, and brethren, and sisters, yea, and his own life also, he cannot be my disciple." The Word also says,

"For which of you, intending to build a tower, sitteth not down first, and counteth the cost, whether he have sufficient to finish it?"

Our assignment is so much bigger than how we feel. You can't trust your emotions when it comes to the price of greatness. I always go back to what God said first. If God gave you a word to complete an assignment, understand that there is a price, a sacrifice to reach completion. So many people abort their assignment based on how they feel. It's not about how you feel, it's not about your friends, it's not even about your family. Yes, God wants you to live your life, but He wants your first priority to be your love for Him and your assignment on this earth. I try to give testimonies to show people this journey isn't for the faint or weak. It's not always going to be a walk through the lily fields. Life is real. The way you get past anything or any situation the enemy has thrown your way is to grab hold of this Scripture in Revelation 12:11: "And they overcame him by the blood of the Lamb, and by the word of their testimony."

By grabbing hold of that Scripture and by allowing it to be a normal part of your life, you are literally snatching the power from the enemy he originally intended to use to bring shame, hurt, and embarrassment by embracing your journey by, empowering yourself and using your story to your advantage. There is a price for greatness; you must pay the cost to be the boss. The key is to always remember that broken crayons still color.

BROKEN – THEN BLESSED!

By Dr. Kanica James

For the most part, people desire to go greater and be blessed. Even though we haven't been to this new level of greatness, we can identify a blessing when we hear it, see it, touch it, taste it, or feel it. The reality is that some will never achieve greater because they often give up the moment they are broken. Brokenness is a state of strong emotional pain that stops someone from living a normal or healthy life. Life can be an adventurous ride of emotions filled with swift transitions and countless ups and downs. You must realize that difficulties will come; the question is: "Are you willing to go through the process?"

There is a mental and spiritual test that is attached to the journey of being a CEO/Entrepreneur. The greater the journey, the greater the test! One minute you're safe and secure. The next minute you may be tumbling head over heels in a metaphorical sense as it seems that your entire world has crumbled to pieces.

This is precisely my story. I can vividly recall a situation when it seemed as though my physical being had just snapped and broke apart, leaving me to fall fast with nothing to support me or stop my tumble. I mean, if it wasn't one thing, it was another. If it's not this, it was certainly that! If the problem wasn't over here, it was over there, and it seemed as if all of hell was breaking loose against me.

I remember going to Bible study because I needed a moment of refreshing. I had anticipated this study all day. I was so eager to fellowship with the congregants that I purchased a light meal for all to enjoy after the study. Halfway through the study, I was pulled out of class and instructed to go to the pastor's office immediately. I proceeded to the pastor's office in an overly chipper fashion. The study was that good! I assumed that the pastor had a quick question or comment and that I'd soon be headed back to the Bible class. Well, I got to the office and was told to have a seat. I knew that I hadn't done anything wrong, so I was puzzled by the serious look on the pastor's face. What could be so important to pull me out of a much-needed motivating Bible class?

I was then informed that a close relative had been molested by my fiancé at the time. I heard what was being said, but I couldn't respond. It seemed like I had entered a twilight zone. I looked at the pastor's wife to gauge her response because I wasn't sure if I was hearing things correctly. When I saw her face, my entire world: my family, my upcoming marriage, my sense of security, and my goals instantly crumbled apart. The room began to spin, and I felt like I was going to pass out. I was numb! I didn't understand how the love of my life could betray me like this. A twenty-two-year relationship ended in a devastating manner, with no closure. I was BROKEN! I couldn't make sense of the matter, and it was a very difficult and lengthy trial that tested my resolve and challenged my faith. How was I supposed to survive this? How could anything good come from this? How am I going to make it through the night, not to mention face the dawning of a new day?

I didn't sleep or eat for weeks. In fact, I don't even remember drinking anything for the first week. I was in shock, and my brain was on auto-pilot. I was engrossed in the matter and so overwhelmed in my thought process that I didn't think to eat. I was killing myself by starvation. There was so much going on in addition to this crisis that I couldn't even pray. I can remember telling myself, "Go to Church; the Word will keep you." I did just that: I went to church. The very place where I received the devastating news. With tear-stained cheeks, I pressed through the shame, guilt, hurt, uncertainties, anger, and frustration to get to the house of God. Since I didn't have the courage to use my God-given measure of strength, I determined to assemble where somebody could pray for me. I was determined to hear what God had to say.

While en route, the song "Greater is Coming" by Jekalyn Carr came on the radio. The lyrics said, "An olive must go through three stages for its oil to run: It has to go through the shaking, the beating, and the pressing. And just like the olive, some of you may have felt like you're going through the shaking, the beating, and the pressing. You've [gone] through all of that for your oil to flow. Now, your greater is coming." As I listened to the song, I understood the direct parallel between the olive harvesting process and life's growing pains. I recognized that if I wanted to go greater and possess the blessings that God had for me, it meant that I had to get rid of everything ungodly and transition into new ways of thinking. I realized that I had poured new wine into an old wineskin, which was causing it to burst. That is to say, I wanted this new life to go greater and be blessed, but I also wanted to hold on to my old ways. Old patterns of thinking and behaving. I was a believer in Christ, desiring to live Holy, yet I was fully okay with making wicked decisions. I was about to enter a marriage unequally yoked but was broken for my own good.

I didn't know that this was for my good during the process. After all, I almost settled for a spouse that looked good on the surface but was full of dead man's bones. What makes matters worse is that when he was confronted with the allegations against him, he didn't leave quietly. He was determined to break me further. He developed an approach designed to tear me down because of his eventual fate. Because of his behaviors, I didn't want to work and lost confidence. I felt that I had no real value left. Though broken, the moment I began to tell my story, I realized that the story was my blessing. God used this brokenness to bless me. I was trying to hold on to the bondage that He [God] wanted to release me from. Through the demise of the relationship with my fiancé, I no longer had to argue concerning my whereabouts; I no longer had to submit my undergarments to prove that I wasn't being sexually immoral. I didn't have to check to see if he was on the couch, dead or drunk. I could now focus wholeheartedly on Kanica and the purpose for which she was created. Those who knew what was going on had pity for me. Several dismissed me, and I was the subject of their gossip. So, I isolated myself until God showed me that this was my purpose. When you are facing a time of brokenness, and it feels as though the emotional pain is more than you can bear, rather than giving up, ask the Lord to reveal what He is teaching you.

Far too often, we regard broken things as despised and insignificant. The truth is that Broken people are not worthless. In fact, it's an opportunity for God to take what has been broken and remake it into something better, something that He can use for His glory. Sin is the underlying cause of broken things and broken people. Nevertheless, God sent His Son, who was without sin, to be broken so that we might be healed. This is a true blessing! Because He was broken, I am blessed.

A crayon can be broken, melted, chipped, shaved, or crushed, and yet it will never lose its color. No matter what you're going through, you were designed for a purpose. That purpose is to leave a positive mark.

BLINDED BY BETRAYAL

by Stephanie West

In the beginning, it was a beautiful connection, it was the help, the assistance, and the business partner I thought I needed, but who would have known that she would rob me, steal my clients, and betray me in the worst way possible. It was a moment where I felt my world tumbling down, but the sweetest revenge would be greater than anything I could ever imagine.

Today, we're going to call her Sandy—why Sandy, I don't know, it just feels right, "lol." So, let's get into it. Sandy and I created a partnership from a business that I had created. It was my business that was already a working process; I just felt it would be great to add some assistance, but later, I found out that it would be seven months of hell. Within that time, Sandy turned an aspiring business that I started from scratch upside down. She stole money from me and took clients from me, and not only that, she had the nerve to leave my business and create her own with my clients, which would be the ultimate betrayal.

Here is where the story gets juicy. All while gaining new clients, making more money, and getting better opportunities, Sandy came to me one day asking if she could take over the finance department, and I thought it would be a great idea, being that it was one less thing I didn't have to worry about—"WRONG." That's when the stealing and lies began, but that's what happens when you trust someone.

The sad thing is, I trusted Sandy, and I really liked her, but when you are dealing with someone with ill intentions, honesty is up for grabs. Before I could realize all the foolery and trickery Sandy was doing, she had already stolen from my company and drained me of a company I had built from the ground up. When it came time for the two of us to get paid, her paycheck was always greater than mine, and with this being the business that I created, the red flags came out. I wanted to know what was going on, and she claimed she had done extra work on the side, which was a complete lie.

Sandy was so used to stealing from my company and lying about it that it became second nature to her, and that was so disgusting. But help me say, "Better days are coming." I thought we had a great work relationship, but sometimes, when you trust people, never knowing that they have agendas, you miss out on the red flags that you may have noticed if you had paid attention before. It's true when they say every dog has its day because I was about to be brought to the light.

Everything hit the fan when an opportunity came knocking that would blow the lid off of the roof and expose this thief. Not only would I be heartbroken, but to know that someone I trusted with my business would betray me—that's the part that hurt me the most because, once again, I trusted Sandy. Since my business had such a good name, companies were always notified of our great work, and that's what kept us in business. But here comes the smoke. There was this lady who wanted to give us an amazing opportunity, but she wanted to see our books, and there she noticed some Tom foolery going on with the business finances.

While going through our business financial books, she wanted to discuss a few things, and that's when I found out all the scheming going on. Not only was she getting paid by my business, but she found a way to receive a second pay cut right up under my nose. I mean, this lady was bold, cold-hearted, and not to mention a plain ole conniving thief. After confronting this little thief about her wrongdoings, Sandy tried turning things around on me, and of course, that didn't end well because she got exposed.

My inner woman wanted to get physical with her, but I'm always a classy lady, and I gave her a pass. I just relieved her of her duties because I'm too cool for the drama and tried to deal with all of the collateral damage she caused my business. What I didn't know is since I let Sandy reside over the finances, she would later wipe my bank account out, steal my clients, and leave me dry.

At this point, it was war because I had nothing. It was like all that I had worked for was gone in a matter of seconds, but an angel would come to my rescue. I would say that I am a good-hearted person, and I try to do right by people, so I believe something good has to happen for me. I was so broken and let down, and I honestly didn't know how I was going to recover, but after praying many nights and asking

God to restore me and my business, I got a call from a new client.

I began working for this new client. I decided to tell him my story and what I had gone through; he was there to listen and hear me out. What I didn't know is that he took everything I said to heart and wanted to help me, so he began promoting me on the radio and introducing me to anyone who could help. It was the blessing I needed when I thought no one was listening, but I tell you this—you can't keep a good-hearted lady down, and from that moment, I never looked back.

Through it all, I learned that when God gives you something, no man can take it away, and no matter how hard someone tries to take it away, "TRUST GOD IN ALL YOUR WAYS" because He will never fail. I want you to know that I still have many hurdles to climb as I walk this journey, but I need you to know to put your trust in God and not man/woman, and you can do it.

Remember, if your dream is to be a millionaire or whatever you desire, you can do it—just keep God first, and He will put you first.

COLORING THROUGH BROKENNESS: FAITH AND RESILIENCE

by Dr. Shelly N. Martin

We all have choices and free will in life. The ability to write our life's narrative depends on our actions and how intentional we are in accomplishing our goals. Research has shown that when we take care of ourselves, we have more clarity, reduce stress, and stay focused. Without self-care, our minds become idle, opening the door to doubt, depression, inadequacy, and negativity. Self-care starts with an unwavering faith-based foundation, positive affirmations and thoughts, and validation. Self-care is an investment in ourselves to help create balance and mental alignment. Everyone must create a self-care plan to take care of the things in life that keep us motivated and going. When we do not invest in self-care, we don't love ourselves enough, making it impossible to share our love with others. It is key that our plans are in full alignment with God so that

He continues to bless the work of our hands and be a blessing to someone else.

Society has placed a stigma on many of us who had to fight for a seat at the table with the expectation of maintaining a "survival of the fittest" mindset. In maintaining the core of our being, we sometimes neglect our needs. Neglecting our needs leaves us feeling unproductive, unfulfilled, and with the need to be relevant. There are many times when we are faced with having to smile through our pain. In leadership, we are often called to be at the height of our game, but we feel unbalanced and defeated. We juggle different aspects of our lives, from family dynamics to job expectations and spiritual walks. We must mask our brokenness with a smile and the words, "I am fine" or "I am blessed and highly favored." Still, in reality, we want to say, "I am weak, I feel broken, and I struggle every day to keep this smile on my face." Vance Havner once said, "God uses broken things. It takes broken soil to produce a crop, broken clouds to give rain, broken grain to give bread, and broken bread to give strength. It is the broken alabaster box that gives forth perfume. It is

Peter, weeping bitterly, who returns to greater power than ever." Even in our brokenness, we are given an assignment to fulfill. Life fulfillment is not in the awards we win along the way, the accolades we receive in life, or the job promotions we acquire as we move along the ladder, but in how we use our talents to serve the people in this world.

A servant's heart is essential to our life's assignment and fulfillment. We may be broken crayons in the box of life, but we still color. I'm reminded of a scripture that says, "Only what you do for Christ will last." So, I often ask myself what the dash in my life means. The dash symbolizes the moments we used our talents to serve, glorify God, and make a difference. Life fulfillment is overcoming many hurdles and obstacles that may be in our way, but walking in God's plans should be our life's strategy. The storms of life may leave you broken and weak, but God gives us the strength to still color. Coloring is alive in your testimony and your perseverance. Through your testimony, your words give encouragement and confirmation.

Life is like a book with chapters. Each chapter represents a lesson that creates a foundation we use to fuel our beliefs, values, and moral compass. The significant chapters typically consist of love, family, career, and spirituality. As we grow, each chapter looks different but should be fully aligned. Entering a new area in the chapter of our book can be scary. Sometimes, we lose our sense of security and familiarity. Sometimes, we are forced to embrace our uniqueness, often taking baby steps as we ease into our new normal while controlling the narrative. We must remember that there is a plan when we enter a new phase. We should also remember that everything works together for good and trust the process. Change is never easy; it takes some reflection and patience. A journey through life has its highs and lows. We must maintain our focus and stay the course to accomplish our life's purpose. If we work and embrace the changes, we can see the beauty in the transformation it brings. While transforming, we may experience heartache, stress, insomnia, and brokenness. We must remember that although we encounter obstacles, our "crayons" may break, but they still color.

In my walk, the box of crayons represents the basket holding life lessons. The "crayons" represent different areas or lessons within the box. Each lesson shaped who I am today. These lessons taught me what I needed to do to be positioned to reach my next level. There were also lessons I needed to experience to clear out distractions preventing me from reaching the next level. Nevertheless, I will continue to be thankful for the knowledge I've acquired along the way because it was God's will. As I reflect on life, I am reminded that despite positive or negative events in our life's journey that may break us and we may reach our lowest point, it doesn't matter how broken our crayons are; we must rise above each challenge and color our pages because it tells our story and shares our blueprint for how we've overcome obstacles. Take your box of crayons and continue to create beautiful pages in life. Don't worry about how broken they may be because your picture is original; it's unique, and it's you.

BROKENNESS TO BEAUTY

by Dr. Yvette McGill

I know broken crayons still color because, for a long time, I used to think that life had me tied up, hemmed up, and laid up in sin's bed, unable to cover my head. Unable to see all life had to offer me. I used to think life had tracked me down generationally so that everything they had done was lying at my feet. I started believing that everything my family was doing or had done was now sitting at my feet. Then, one day, I was reminded that Christ won back at Calvary. He rewrote my DNA, changed my name, gave me HIS identity, and changed my name. I am everything that GOD says I am—a usable crayon. I spent most of my life wishing I was dead, to the point where, as a mother and wife, I was begging GOD to take my life every day.

Now let me explain to you why I'm considered a broken crayon—because with all that has happened to me, I know GOD still sees me as usable for the kingdom, and for that, I'm grateful. Let me explain...

At the age of 25, God had me go to my mom and give her forgiveness, and I always liked to tell people I was just obedient ENOUGH to do it. Truly, I did not understand why, and I did question God as to why I needed to give her forgiveness instead of her asking me for forgiveness. Once I did, I actually thought that was very kind of me to do, not knowing years later it was for my own good. You see, 25 years later, I would be 50 years old, and GOD then told me to go to my 25-year-old daughter and ask for forgiveness. From this lesson, GOD taught me the importance of obeying His directions. HE actually told me that if I hadn't given my mom forgiveness, He would not have allowed my daughter to forgive me.

At that point in life, you could not have convinced me that I was no longer usable, but I was wrong, and I'm so very thankful I was. As a matter of fact, this is truly a moment where I was able to see that I was still usable. GOD had me leave my corporate

America job of 23 years, pull out all my money, and open a daycare. Now, mind you, I always wanted a daycare where I would take care of newborns, but I had no interest in any other age group. Well, I quickly found out I had to offer more than just a center for newborns; I had to offer services for all ages. Then GOD said, go and ask your daughter to join you. I did, and she said yes. Now, it was not as quick as this sounds, but for the sake of speeding up this story, she said yes. So, I got everything together with the state, and let's just say that by itself, it was not EASY. So many times, I just wanted to run back to my job and forget what GOD told me to do, but there were many factors that would not allow this. One huge one was that I had allowed my daughter to pull my grandson out of daycare, and I agreed to take care of him until she was able to quit her job and join me. When I tell you we had a priceless moment, a moment that is still rewarding me today—it was that and more. Finally, there came a time when my daughter joined me, and we had three beautiful days that could have only happened at the hand of GOD. When I say beautiful, I use that word in the sense of who GOD is, knowing full well that those three years were filled with every emotion GOD gives to man. There were times when we did not speak or talk to each other, and then there were other days when we laughed, prayed, and played with the children we were responsible for. Needless to say, GOD knew what HE was doing. I was not quite sure, but one thing was for sure: I had come to understand that I was still a usable crayon, to say the least.

I became a mother to many and a grandmother, better known as Mimi, to others. Now, Mimi was my name for Khi, but after saying over and over to the other children that I was their Mimi, he finally decided to share me with the daycare babies. By the time GOD gave me direction to close the doors of the daycare, I was hooked and found it hard to say goodbye. It was in October 2019 that GOD told me that the mission was accomplished, and as much as I knew what He was saying, I ignored His directions. It was in December 2019, when I went to meet with my new editor for my new book project, that I realized GOD was not playing with me. The editor was also a Pastor, and before our meeting ended, she said, "Ms. Yvette, I must tell you, GOD said until you close that door, He cannot release His blessing on this project." She asked me if I knew what He meant, and I said yes. I drove back to my daycare in complete silence, knowing I had to do the unthinkable and tell my babies I had to close my doors. Again, this was another moment when I was just obedient enough to do what HE said so HE could bless me as HE intended to do. During that time, I used my anger control knowledge and skills to counsel many parents, even those who chose not to enroll their children with me; they still thanked me for the conversation we had... another "used crayons still color" episode.

Last but not least, I thank GOD I'm a usable crayon, and I still feel as though I have a lot to do on this earth. I want to do it EVERY DAY to the fullest. I'm now a motivational speaker, and I love exchanging my truth for others' transformation, which is the name of my first book, #theEXCHANGE. As a result of me no longer being full of anxiety and depression, I was able to clearly hear from GOD and write a book that changed the trajectory of my life and generations to come. My grandson now walks in the truth of who he is, something

I was not strong enough to give my daughter, his mom. A lot of people decided not to deal with me, but GOD sent all the right people to love me, mold me, and accept me with all my flaws. I'm now a successful author, motivational speaker, life coach, and anger specialist—all because I decided to see value in myself. I'm proud to be a broken crayon that still colors because it is within my brokenness that I'm able to help others see that no matter what you do or go through, GOD still sees value in your life, and although some people may quit on you, NEVER, and I do mean NEVER quit on yourself. The best part of my life happened once I allowed GOD to break me.

Signed, #theEXCHANGE

Made in the USA
Monee, IL
26 February 2025